MAHABHARATA
STORIES

The Palace of Lac

Subhadra Sen Gupta

Om KIDZ
An imprint of Om Books International

Dhritarashtra had very reluctantly made Yudhishthira the crown prince because his subjects wanted it. He was very disappointed because he had wished his eldest son Duryodhana to follow him to the throne.

Shakuni, Duryodhana and Dusshasana decided the only way that they could hold on to power was to get rid of the Pandavas.

Duryodhana said to Shakuni, “We cannot kill the Pandavas in a fighting contest because they will surely defeat us.”

Dusshasana warned, “They will have to die in such a way that no one suspects us. The Pandavas are very popular with the people who will be angry if we are caught.”

Shakuni smiled, “Leave it all to me, my nephews. The Pandavas will die and everyone will think it is an accident.”

Shakuni called the architect named Purochana and gave him the plan for a new palace.

Shakuni said, "I want you to build a palace with material that will catch fire very quickly. The walls and roof should be made of lac."

Chief Minister Vidura was passing by when he heard Shakuni talking to Purochana and was very puzzled. "A palace of lac! Why does Shakuni want a palace that can catch fire? I don't trust him. He is planning something!"

The palace of lac was built by Purochana and it was a very beautiful building. People saw the new palace and praised it, not knowing it was made for a very cruel purpose.

Purochana said to Shakuni, "The palace is ready, Your Highness."

Shakuni laughed, "I am very pleased!"

Duryodhana invited the Pandavas and Kunti to a feast at the new palace.

Kunti said happily, "This is a beautiful building Duryodhana. Who will stay here?"

Duryodhana replied, "You will, Your Majesty. I have built it for you and my Pandava brothers."

As the Pandavas were happily planning to live in a palace of their own, Vidura hurried to meet them. Vidura warned Kunti, "Please do not go to that palace. Your lives will be in danger there."

Kunti was puzzled, "How can our lives be in danger Vidura?"

Vidura then explained, "I had heard Shakuni talking to Purochana. He instructed Purochana to make the building with material like lac, jute and ghee so that it would catch fire easily."

Hearing that the palace was made of lac and a plan to kill them was being hatched, Bhima became very angry and shouted, "The Kauravas think that they can kill us? I am going to kill them first!"

Vidura stopped Bhima from going off to attack Duryodhana saying, "We have to be clever and fool the Kauravas. They must think you all are dead and then you can take revenge later."

Yudhishthira asked, "Then what should we do? We have promised Duryodhana that we will live in the palace."

Then Vidura suggested a plan. "You must first go to live in the palace. Then you have to escape in secret so that the Kauravas think you have all perished in the fire."

Vidura went on, “Dig a secret tunnel under the palace that leads to the forest far away and then when they set the palace on fire you can all escape. And hide in the forest against the army of Duryodhana.”

The Pandavas secretly dug a tunnel and prepared to escape.

Arjuna said to his brothers, “We will live in the forest in disguise as a poor family. No one should find out that we are the royal princes of Hastinapur or our life will be in danger.”

Bhima nodded, “I agree. If our uncle Dhritarashtra finds out that we are alive, he will surely send his sons to kill us.”

One night, Duryodhana's men set the palace of lac on fire. The Pandavas and Kunti quickly entered the tunnel and escaped into the forest where they could not be found easily.

Dhritarashtra and his sons believed that the Pandavas and Kunti were dead.